Secret Balancing Act

Keep Your Balance

Secret Balancing Act

Keep Your Balance

GEOFFREY ZAMBONI

Published in the United States of America

ISBN 979-8-89395-163-9 (SC)
ISBN 979-8-89395-165-3 (HC)
ISBN 979-8-89395-164-6 (Ebook)

Library of Congress Control Number: 2025910173

Geoffrey Zamboni Publishing
145 W Broadway
Long Beach, CA 90802, USA
www.stellarliterary.com

Order Information and Rights Permission:

Quantity sales. Special discounts might be available on quantity purchases by corporations, associations, and others. For details, contact the publisher at the address above.

For Book Rights Adaptation and other Rights Permission.
Call us at toll-free 1-888-945-8513 or send us an email at
admin@stellarliterary.com.

Contents

Prologue

Life as we know isn't, contrary to the seemingly normal approach, about how much we can accumulate or about what we do for a living. The irony of this is that unless one has some life altering experience which forces you to look at your own mortality, we continue down the same path without thought to the real beauty of life…those people around us who complete our lives. Without giving back, we just take up space and resources.

This attempt to chronicle the life altering impact of many things in my life and in the lives of those I love will hopefully give some insight into what I firmly believe is the real part of life. Everything we 'own,' everything we 'have,' either rusts, breaks or is eventually recycled back into the world. The only thing of merit we can claim as truly ours is the love, honesty, and compassion with which we live our lives. That, in the final analysis, is what is left of our life on this planet. Whether those qualities are manifested in books, plays, and poems or simply in the memory of those we touch that, to me at least, is what makes us a success.

Ironic, isn't it? Some of us are fortunate enough to have parents or mentors of some sort who give us the ability to look beyond ourselves. Most of us, however, either due to life's little surprises or being pulled by one ear kicking and screaming, only see the beauty and the true reality of life by getting our nose firmly rubbed in it. I sometimes think I wasn't given the owner's manual for this vehicle called a soul and body. But then, the awe and wonder of suddenly seeing something profound for the first time would be lost, wouldn't it? The wonder of the realization of love and trust in someone's eyes looking back at you is one of those things. Do you pull back or open up? It seems to me that is the 'make or break' point in many of our lives…and can you be honest with that person? …can you ***let*** yourself be loved?

All of us must balance our lives – juggling professions against personal life, families, health and peace of mind. For many of us, we are in denial about needing to do this making our *Balancing Act* a Secret even from ourselves.

This book tells of some of those 'ear-pulling' struggles with my life and others.

Geoffrey Zamboni

Introduction

Dedication. Perseverance. Compassion. Integrity.

You would not think of these terms as traits that would be undesirable or problematic, would you? Yet, the irony is that these are some of the attributes which, when added to situational issues (e.g., overworking, unreasonable deadlines, having feelings of no control, lack of balance in one's life), can cause professional and personal burnout to such a degree as to result in a type of subtle clinical depression now found in many people whose lifestyles or jobs would be categorized as high stress.

Often viewed as a sign of weakness, especially in men, the factors involved here manifest themselves in a multitude of symptoms. Only a few of these symptoms are CFS (chronic fatigue syndrome), irritability, lack of patience and an ever-increasing desire to shut out the world. The salient issue here is that not only is this process such an insidious thing that by the time it is recognized it is severe; but that merely admitting to it on any level, openly or internally, is viewed as a clear sign of failure personally and professionally. Therefore, the tendency is to not to even acknowledge that there is a problem but hide it at ***any*** cost. I know from personal experience that, having recognized this on some visceral level and refusing (or being unable) to deal with it, I suffered more than I would have had I come out into the daylight with it. At one point it could have cost me my profession and nearly my marriage.

I had to get out to survive.

Many of us who experience this process are overachievers who would never think to 'drop out' much less even temporarily jump off the proverbial fast track. Therefore, we treat the worst days as an anomaly and tell ourselves, "OK, so I'm having a bad day today. Get OVER it. I'll just have to work harder." On the least symptomatic of the 'problem' days we might dimly realize we are not quite as effective as we could be. Each of us might feel this process in varying degrees of intensity depending on the day, our personal make-up, our level of affliction, our support systems and/or our level of internal accountability. The cumulative numbers of years without a break under this type of stress, can – among other things –induce serotonin depletion. It may also be a determining factor in the severity of this condition.

While I have held administrative positions in health care, for the record, I am not a physician, clinician nor do I have a medical school degree. I am merely one of the walking wounded. The ideas, feelings and theories outlined herein are only based on my observations and experiences in my own life and come out of living through this.

For the purposes of this book, I will call this problem CDB or "corporate depressive burnout". I have come to believe that CDB is far more common than many of us realize. I hope that there will be, finally, a new school of thought showing it as a corporate problem as opposed to being a weakness in a person's make-up. While this will not be endorsed unilaterally, this recognition would, at the very least, be a start.

Finally recognizing this problem is quite like buying a particular type of car and then suddenly noticing how many people drive the same kind of vehicle. Those vehicles were always there; however, we were in denial and unaware. Likewise, our desensitization to personal issues only exacerbates this problem as, being insidious, it normally isn't noticed for years or we attribute the symptoms as a normal response to the stress and demands of our professions and our hyper-speed lives. I seriously doubt that any of you reading this have not had at least one of these thoughts at some point in your career. *"Why am I having a problem dealing with routine daily tasks?" "So, what makes me any different (read: inferior)?" "I can't (don't' dare!) admit I'm feeling ANY sort of compromise in my ability to cope."*

My sincere hope is that this book will not only be a wake-up call for many who are unable or unwilling to admit that they have a problem but will also let others know that they are not alone…AND it is not a personality flaw nor a weakness in any sense of the word. Hopefully, there may be a person out there who reads this and is able to make some changes in his or her life before the burnout happens and affects the rest of their lives.

As important as the other key issues, the other underlying hope is that managers will be more observant of their employees and the environment in which they put them.

In these hard-economic times, I will wager that this syndrome will be even more prevalent as those who have jobs will not want to lose them at any cost...even that of one's health and family.

Balance. That is such a loaded word. In our lives, it means keeping perspective. It means understanding you cannot be everything to everybody at the cost of your happiness, that of your spouse's happiness and most importantly your health. So, we work in denial of needing this balance...hence: our *Secret Balancing Act.*

Thank you for reading.

Geoffrey Zamboni

Palm Desert, California

Chapter 1
I Want Out

"What in the hell is happening to me?"

I sat at my desk in the middle of an afternoon finding myself disoriented, irritable and wanting to shove all the paperwork on my desk into the wastebasket. It was a feeling I was unable to define, although, if I were honest, I knew that this had been coming for some time. I had noticed, in recent weeks, that I was cutting conversations short, not listening fully, and becoming frustrated with normal everyday problems in the hospital. I had just come from a staff meeting where several department managers ambushed me. I knew I had been set up and was naïve enough not to have seen it coming. This same trio had succeeded some months ago in getting our initial director of nursing fired.

Although this situation was many years ago, I have very recently experienced it yet again and, eerily, the same feelings surfaced. The situation with being ambushed happened again. Having taken a position which had no one in a formal management position for five prior years, the system was rife with problems. Additionally, with a complicated patient delivery system, staff issues, having to reconstruct P&P manuals, which were never really in existence and having providers asking me to sit in with patients due to many issues, time was at a premium each day. A staff IT person went to our executive director advising him I had put the agency in jeopardy by not completing a survey on schedule. He was upset thinking I had purposefully hidden this issue. I had admitted that to her in a meeting but also told her that I had been in constant touch with the program director for that survey who advised me that although I had missed a formal deadline, if I got the survey done by the end of that month, there was no real problem. He said that they put that kind of deadline out to allow for this type of situation. I completed the survey advising the ED who gave me a 'high five'. I am not sure if that says I am too naïve and trusting, or that the same kind of personality still exists in business...probably both. One would think I would have learned from the first experience.

Early on, I was the second person hired to open what turned into a major cancer center, later receiving National Cancer Institute designation. Immediately after opening, we had just come through a very rough start-up and finally had patients in our hospital. No less than ten construction delays, multiple staffing problems, MANY program changes, substantial equipment modifications and months of sleep deprivation had brought all of us away from the excitement of opening this hospital and into the reality of departmental politics and self-serving attitudes. The pressures of having come through this were telling on all of us. What had been camaraderie was quickly disintegrating into open hostility at times. Our board meetings as well as department head meetings had become shouting matches and even at times obvious petty political ploys for the "Give me the glory" now that we were seeing patients.

This was the culmination of nearly two years of sixteen to eighteen-hour days. I was thinking, *God, was all that worth THIS*?

During the nine-month period just prior to opening, I had lost both my grandmothers, my mother was giving an Oscar-winning performance as

Camille and I had lost a dearly beloved pet of fourteen years. I tried putting all that in focus, telling myself *"OK, listen. You were an integral part in opening a major hospital. It opened. It is working. It is no small feat and one which few professionals get to do. So, you are stressed!! Big deal. Get OVER yourself."*

Shortly after opening this facility, the opportunity to move into a different sector of patient care was offered and I took it thinking I needed a change and that, although still part of the same physician's group, being in a different environment would recharge my batteries. For the first several years, it seemed to be exactly what I needed. As time went on and my responsibilities increased, I began to feel many of the same things all over again. Granted, they were more subtle and therefore less recognizable, but nevertheless lurked just below the surface.

Toward the end of that phase of my career, the one from which I retired (should I say left in the dust), I had become reclusive, irritable, and very tired most of the time. As with any health care delivery system, we have been hit with multiple sets of financial constraints, the least of which was to reduce overhead and worst of which was the mandate to reduce staff. Adding to the dysfunction, several key players left, including our director of nursing allowing an opening for a very controlling, self-serving individual to be hired on staff in a key administrative position.

There is not any section of corporate America that has not had and does not have those issues. Bear in mind, however, that a patient care delivery system is not an office where if someone is out for a day, the work can be put on hold. Reducing staff and services means compromising care in some form, be it ever so subtle...or not. In that environment, when you reduce anything in any area without proper planning, changing demographics, someone else must pick up the slack and run with it. It puts tremendous pressure on professionals with integrity to keep on performing. It was with this ongoing scenario that I was unable to cope.

The pivotal day, although I had no idea at the time of its significance, was a day nearly three months before the final revelation hit me and I knew I had to get out. I had finished making rounds and was on the way back to my office when I got a page from one of my front-line staff members. As I entered my outer office, a physician with whom I had had a running battle with about his staff performance and finances followed me in. I motioned for him to have a seat in the outer office while I made the phone call to answer the page.

When I picked up the phone, I heard the warbling sound indicating that I had a voice mail. I had cleared nearly twenty voice mails that morning, most of which had problems attached to them. Upon hearing that irritating noise, I was overcome by a form of frustration and rage that quite unnerved me. I think I basically blanked out for a second. I know that, had the physician not been behind me in my outer office, I might have ripped the cord out of the wall and given the phone a premature death. Instead, I took several deep breaths, thankful that he could not see my face and made the call delegating the problem. Hanging up the phone I motioned for him to come in. We ended up having an unscheduled two-hour meeting about many issues, during which time, my lapse of control became further and further a distant unpleasant memory.

In the following weeks, I completely forgot about that incident and immersed myself in my job once again. I loved what I did. The constant changes and challenges seemed to suit my personality. I just did not know that my credit had run out and the price I was now paying was putting me further in the red daily.

Color me naive, I still loved my job.

I recall one day when a code blue was called in our outpatient parking lot at eight in the morning. A patient had come to our facility as a referral from a local community doc. We later found out that the physician should probably have admitted his patient to the hospital the day before. As he got out of his car, he lost consciousness. Fortunately, my parking lot staff immediately noticed him fall and radioed in for a code.

After two hours, a loss of heart activity for over two minutes, countless chest compressions and defibrillator shocks, he was barely stable enough to transport to the emergency room. As he was put in the back of the ambulance, one of the medics was straddled across his stomach still performing compressions. The parking lot looked like a war zone with gloves and various wrappers strewn all over the place. Three EMS ambulances had converged on the scene and four of our doctors and six nurses performed the miracle of keeping this poor soul alive.

Our QA (quality assurance) meeting later that day confirmed we had done all we could and did it to the best of our abilities. I left that day feeling elated that our team was so good. Seeing the staff interact so well with each other was like seeing a precision piece of equipment run. I finished the reports, took care of some last-minute phone calls, and headed home early that night at 7pm. I was told that day I looked like hell. Thinking it was just evidence of working hard, I jokingly said, "Why thank you." After I got home and took a dip in the pool and had dinner, I crashed. The next day I was so tired I had to force myself to get up and move around. It was Saturday and we did the usual home stuff. I retired early that night and awoke Sunday feeling refreshed. So, I said to myself, you just needed a day off and a good night's rest. I worked at home Sunday, took a quick run to the hospital for some papers and after a half hour's work at my desk returned home to a quiet Sunday evening. By Monday afternoon I felt as though I had not slept all weekend. I pushed it off, ignoring the gathering cloud and got on with my day. *Hell*, I told myself, *it was just one of 'those' days. Get over it.*

Three months later I found myself facing off with a physician in the middle of a patient treatment zone about an issue he had handled badly. Normally able to be firm and diplomatic, I was close to maniacal and began realizing that I was drawing the wrong kind of attention not only from our staff but from patients as well. The physician was a resident and new to being somewhat on his own. I should have been far more understanding; however, he had written a script for the wrong medications for a patient. Adding to the problem, he blamed his nurse. After correcting him, he blamed the inaccuracy of the medical record…then he blamed the system. I advised him about patient safety and his charge to "do no harm" then remembered raising my voice to a level I did not use and all activity around us stopped. To add insult to injury, this problem was brought to me by one of our vice-presidents as it was his wife for whom we were caring. She had presence enough to check the script. While this was serious, I should have handled it much differently.

Returning to my office, I closed my office door and sat at my desk in a stupor. My administrative assistant was gone, and the place was quiet. Suddenly overcome by a bone deep fatigue, I put my head down on my desk. The flood of feelings and memories of those days of opening the hospital, all the feelings of betrayal (real and imagined), the overwhelming sense of frustration of those days and this immediate time hit me with a vengeance. Up out of this vortex of feelings came the realization that if I continued in this direction, I would no longer be effective at what I was doing. I was scared.

I heard my admin return. I walked out and told her I was taking the rest of the day off and could not be reached. She was visibly shocked but, seeing my face, did not ask for any other information.

I drove to a nearby park and found a secluded spot overlooking the water. I sat there for an hour or more! Numb. Not feeling. Being unable to think. Suddenly I found myself crying uncontrollably. The sobs came from a place that scared the hell out of me.

I knew I had to get out.

Chapter 2
Glimpses

During the immediate period prior to my 'problem', a key vice president who was a mentor of mine had resigned and my director of nursing had also left, leaving me with both of their jobs for a period.

Ironically, the VP left because he knew what was happening to him. Our director of nursing was burned out. He and I had had many conversations about the futility and frustration of our jobs and the effect on our personalities. He often said that staying in any job over five years was a never a good thing as you lose perspective.

Our facility was no different than any other medical care delivery system these days – or any other industry for that matter. We were going through changes in staffing, programming, budgets and suffering the consequences. We all felt the increased tension and loss of morale. Everyone was called upon to do even more than they had previously which was already taxing. Deadlines were unreasonable and often at the whimsy of the board and senior vice-presidents. Staffing had already undergone one round of cuts.

More than one time I prevailed on my staff to complete data for that MOST important report only to see it tabled or even worse, lost in the "system" leaving me unable to later give credence to why it was even an issue. It seemed no one, least of all me, had little or no patience left. I always feel like parroting that line from a Seinfeld show when I get into this: Yadda, yadda, yadda and yadda. It is a broken record…one that organizations keep on playing over and over.

Sitting in a directors meeting one day, trying to force myself to act interested, I realized our CFO was speaking. I could not believe what I was hearing. He was proposing a 'cost cutting' move to save space by removing front line managers from our outpatient facility and placing them one half mile across the street at an office building we had rented for the administrative staff offices, thus freeing the space for physician's offices.

I reacted viscerally and heard myself say, "That is THE stupidest thing I think I have ever heard." After several gasps around the table, all eyes turned to me. He was at first shocked and then you could see the anger literally lashing from his eyes. I knew he was not used to someone challenging him much less addressing him in that fashion. I held his gaze and proceeded, in a calmer manner, to address five compelling reasons why that was not a good idea. The tension began to evaporate in the room; however, the anger still stayed in his eyes. I had made an enemy in a fashion I never would have let happen years ago.

The landmarks, or sometimes landmines, are so often overlooked in haste or in the simple need to put an unpleasant situation behind us. I had been inappropriate and very unprofessional...truthful, but inappropriate. I paid a price for that outburst in that it was months before he and I could once again interact civilly and constructively. It was one more glimpse into that vortex and turmoil just below my consciousness over which I had no control. It seemed to be swirling in an ever-tightening circle around me these days.

This process of self-examination is often painful and often fraught with denial. Even now, as I am writing this, I must fight to get the words out. This path takes us on a journey of self-discovery we quite honestly do not want to make. All the team building seminars, the management seminars and every level of educational courses do not practically prepare us for handling this type of burnout and all its ramifications. I think that I was more willing to admit that I was burning out than I was willing to admit I was not well. The stigma that attends this issue is a huge hurdle to jump.

One of the first symptoms I really noticed was that the inanest things irritated me.

The last and ongoing symptom (to this day) was my chronic and debilitating fatigue, which controlled me so forcefully and completely making a normal day difficult at times. To the surprise of guests at my home (and the ire of my spouse), I would sometimes disappear and later be found on the bed sleeping...I had no choice.

Nothing prepared me for the gut-wrenching soul searching I had to do simply to keep my head above water. Never in my wildest imagination did I even come close to thinking I would have to literally drop out in order to survive. That was the hardest decision in my life. The irony is that it was not a choice. I had none. I was at the wall and the hounds were already taking chunks of flesh. Was it not for a solid personal relationship with my spouse, I do not know where I would be today? I am one of the fortunate ones.

Nothing prepared me for or even gave me a glimmer of the possibility of this thing's existence...or its power over me. Of all the fallout from this process, the most terrible feeling I had was one of being totally out of control. The burn out syndrome is alluded to and often even discussed.

However, being there and feeling the sense of failure, professionally and personally, that accompanies it is not discussed around the water cooler. It is seldom even discussed in annual evaluations. IF it is discussed, it rests on the employee's side of the desk, not the manager's and does not rest with corporate. It is left at best for a therapist's office and at worst, for a bartender's ear…after the damage is done.

Drs. Christina Maslach and Michael Leiter give credible insight to this issue in their book *The Truth About Burnout*. After having read it, I wished it were a required part of every organization's P&P manual. I think all of us get sucked into the process of "getting ahead" and losing our sense of self in order to succeed and live the good life.

The weeks and months before and after I left my job passed with me feeling as though I was alternately riding a roller coaster or walking the beach on a stormy afternoon. I was so torn with feelings of failure and depression that I literally closed off the world, including my interaction with my partner. He later thought I was losing my mind or had taken on the Alzheimer's problems my father had developed in his last years.

During the months before I quit, I began to realize I had a severe problem, I forced myself to work each day. There were many days that I literally locked myself in my office, stared at the paperwork on my desk in a stupor and only returned phone calls after someone left a voice mail. I was becoming ineffective. Even then, I refused to acknowledge I was falling into the pit. It was inconceivable that I could stop functioning and I was in denial that I had a problem. I started each day with a resolve to put this gargoyle in its place and ended most days with it sitting on my shoulder. Looking back, it is amazing to me that such denial can take over an intelligent person to such an extent that, even when daily functioning is minimally effective and at best, he continues to tell himself it is just a phase and will get over it.

These insights and epiphanies are akin to walking fast down a corridor passing various windows looking into a room full of people shouting and arguing uncontrollably. Each time you pass a window, you are amazed at the sight, but you are moving so fast that the effect is surreal, and the impact does not register. Occassionally, you get an insight as you pass one of the windows that something is very wrong with that picture. Once in a great while, you might see yourself in the middle of the fray as a principal character in the performance realizing only for an instant that what is wrong is that you see yourself out of control in the middle of that melee. It is these glimpses which we deny while we are on this journey of unwanted self-discovery.

There were many days during this period where I was effective, praised for my work and felt fine. I was my normal self. I would analyze my 'off days' thinking I was merely fatigued or that I needed to take a different approach to this or that problem. I would tell myself that, if I had handled that problem just a little differently or delegated the other problem out effectively, I would have been far more effective and not had a problem.

All managers who care about their staff and their jobs have strong feelings about process and being fair. We take a lot on ourselves to compensate for the idiosyncrasies of our corporate culture so that it does not impact our staff adversely. The simple fact is that the corporation has a "culture" of its own and, few people really have control of the impact on its staff. It is this feeling of lack of control which is part of the problem and results in an insidious form of stress which then manifests itself in such a way to cause frustration, burn out and feelings of ineffectiveness.

Business today is ego driven rather than service driven. By that I mean that upper managers seem to lose sight of that fact that the business is not about their own success but the success of those who are the front-line employees. We, as managers, are only as good as those who work for us. In creating the policies and procedures they feel will enhance the business, even if seemingly done from an altruistic point of view "to get a more positive bottom line," very few policy makers consult or use the experience of the employees who implement the process. They seldom, if ever, work a full day in their employee's shoes. The problem this creates, both for the upper manager and the front-line employee is that this situation produces an environment wherein the goals are not always attainable or understood...nor are they realistic.

Few corporations or businesses, especially from an HR standpoint, take into consideration the fact that they may have hired an employee into a job for which he or she is not actually suited. Even that 'appropriate' degree and CV will not always be the indication that a person is suited for the job. When confronted with a having made a wrong choice, it is seldom, if ever, the corporation's problem, but the employee's. Add to the mix the inherent expectation to perform we put on our employees and ourselves and you get a potentially volatile problem. Upper-level managers are not always suited for a position even though their education...and in some respects their actual experience would dictate differently. Personality factors hugely into how well managers function and ultimately how the business functions. This, in my experience, is seldom if ever addressed directly, but it is often brought up after the fact or behind closed doors.

It is these 'glimpses' about which we are in denial. Years later it was still difficult to admit that I was still prone to this anomaly.

I had the good fortune to be recruited as director of medical services for an agency with a severely ill population. I say "good fortune" because it was time to give back...to try again. I know I ended up helping many patients get into and stay in care and, I know I saved some lives. I would like to think I had the respect of my staff...well, 'nearly' all of them. That is one thing about a manager's job. It is not a popularity contest. Therein lays any manager's Achilles heel. As good as I can be, and I think like many others, I fall into the trap of wanting to be liked.

Again, as if I had not even been paying attention to the last 30 years, I found myself deep into the daily mix of personality versus work ethic. What is it about over-achievers that put them at odds with balancing their lives? Why do we keep on doing what we do...*wrong*? I have talked to many colleagues, past and present, who give me this look telling me what I am saying goes to the core of their life...and yet...the march goes on.

That epiphany we all get never seems to stay long enough to be recorded...just passes as a dark cloud you are glad to see go away. A glimpse into that vortex is frightening and one we unconsciously choose to ignore as best we can...

Chapter 3
I Won't Own This

Denial. That word takes on a whole new dimension after you're able to finally admit you have been in a hole of your own making.

Those of us who have too much pride, too much of a work-ethic or simply too much of a competitive edge are the last to admit we are in that hole…even when you can no longer raise yourself high enough to see out…even when there are things crawling on the walls.

I refused to look back. On some level I knew that there was this huge gargoyle creeping up on me. I believe I was afraid to look because I knew he would not only consume me, but first he'd scare the hell out of me. The secret I had been hiding had become the proverbial elephant in the middle of the room. This cannot be happening to me. I have too much control, self-respect and I am really a good person. How in the hell did I get here? I'm good at what I do.

My days had taken on a surreal quality at times. I was moving through this mist and at the end of the day I was exhausted to the point of shutting out the rest of the world as well as my spouse. Being a good communicator in business does not always allow the luxury of communicating well with your other half…and *especially* not with yourself. You are the last person in that line-up. The queue goes for blocks and you wonder at times why you are even in the line much less where...

One of the things I love about health care is that you do not know from one minute to the next what lies around the corner or who or what problem is on the end of the next telephone call or voice mail. Ironically, ADD does seem to help with this profession. The downside to all of this happens when you are understaffed you must watch your budget too closely and the "emergencies" take up the day with things you cannot let go as they demand attention 'now'. Only a few of these from my last job are: the crying patient at the front desk, the doctor who suddenly asks you to room the patient with him as there are severe problems with communication and care issues - and that visit takes over an hour of your time, the drug using patient you have to ask to come back for another visit because he just 'shot up' and do not forget the patient you need to get into care who is non-compliant with medications. The worst part of that scenario is that if you are in a management position, there are always projects and deadlines which do not take into consideration the fact that if you are to deliver good care, it takes time and most often face to face contact with patients. Even your peers at times do not understand the level of one on one involvement needed to cope with those kinds of days.

Add to that mix a staff who had no administrator for a very long period who never took the time to not only to work with them for team building/morale issues but who was never in the trenches watching quality assurance and procedural issues.

Opening the hospital was the most wonderful and demanding thing I had ever done...but would never attempt again. The months of sleepless nights, catching forty winks on a gurney in a hallway and the endless rounds of meetings took their toll...and yet I would not give up. I thought that once I left that environment, I would recover... How wrong I was.

This albatross that many of us have on our shoulder can go away for a while if things are easily manageable. But let the stress of being unable to control your days show up and that thing flies back, uninvited, with flapping wings and loud raucous noises when you least expect it.

Such was the recent bout with my nemesis. As with many organizations and businesses these days, everyone wears many hats. The effect of that is it takes so little for that gargoyle to rear its ugly head again.

I had taken on this latest position on a whim and felt pretty good about being able to get back into a management position...and more importantly, into one with such a calling...

The strange thing is that you would think one would learn from earlier trauma. I did...at first. I had this idea that I would work from 8am to 5pm... Well, ok, *maybe* 6pm.

It is ironic that our egos get in the way of our common sense and our professional approach to our jobs. The 'bucket of water syndrome' shows up again and again. We take on these jobs and then tell ourselves, once the crescendo reaches ear-splitting levels, what a great sound.

I began to realize, at too late a date that I am not my job. I work at that. Take for example you have a bucket of water in your office. While it is there, you can put your hand in it, splash water all over the room. Even taking your hand out for a moment, you will still see evidence of your hand having been there. If, however, you leave that bucket (and that job) what happens to the water? It becomes very calm...as though you were never there. We are not our jobs; however, we sure make ourselves wear that cloak.

As with my other job, I had begun to feel tired and sometimes quite frustrated as there was so much to do and accomplish with fewer and fewer resources. The staff overall was great with very few exceptions. I think one of the downfalls of us overachievers, is that we don't delegate well. We always want to be front and center...and in denial that we need to place the responsibility squarely on the shoulders of the person in that job function within our oversight...not control...in place.

I refused to acknowledge, if I am honest about it, that the gargoyle was making these arcs sweeping ever lower above my life. I kept refusing to believe he had left his spot on the top edge of the cathedral.

Chapter 4
Fear

This is probably the hardest chapter to write. Drilling down into this dark abyss is difficult. It means dredging up so many of the things about which I was in denial.

I remember the first time I even came close to realizing what was happening. It scared me and I slammed that door. In the months and years ahead, as I passed that closed door, I had this horrible sense of dread. I knew that one day I'd have to open it and those gargoyles would have at me.

My life was beginning to unravel in that I was having trouble focusing even on even the smallest issues of a normal day. I was hoping the ADD was kicking in, but I was in such denial about it that I refused to even open that door a crack.

Being pushed by budget constraints, along with a very politically driven upper management cadre of people who were more interested in their careers than delivering quality care, did not help with the base problem at all. In fact, it exacerbated not only my ability to effectively do my job but caused some program issues that compromised patient care.

I think every manager has "that" employee who, for whatever reason, continually throws nails in the road hoping to blow your tires. Resentment, I think, plays a big part in a lot of this behavior. Being younger never helps when you are suddenly supervising employees half again your age. Having to write them up is always a challenge.

I think as a manager one must cross the street and look back objectively. It is most difficult when you must make hard decisions. Over the course of my career I have had to relieve several physicians of their positions and write up others. Wishing that I could retrace my steps is futile as that obviously is not on the table.

Being afraid to make these decisions which impact the lives of people you know and work with is understandable…however, necessary at times.

My biggest issue was I tended to care too much about people's feelings and I often gave them the benefit of the doubt. It was hard to put on the "boss" face and deal with someone I knew was having personal problems and it was affecting their work.

Chapter 5
Corporate Mantra

The Good Manager:

> Always knows what goes on in the department.
>
> Should have more technical expertise than any subordinate.
>
> Should be able to solve any problem that comes up.
>
> Should be primary...if not, THE only...person responsible for the quality issues.

Heroes often get tossed in front of the bus.

"OK, folks, what's going to be the focus here? Who wants to begin?"

How many of you have been in team building meetings and heard, if not those words, some remarkably similar?

The last one I attended was to reverse some rather destructive morale which had been in place many years before my arrival. The immediate effect was good; however, noticeably short lived. I was complimented by all my staff and my boss. We all seemed to be able to generate cooperation in that environment away from the workplace itself. As Drs. Christina Maslach and Michael Leiter state – in their book *The Truth About Burnout* - "A person's behavior in the workplace can only be understood when it is examined within the social context of that workplace". I often think that management looks too closely at the individual without enough consideration to the dynamics of both the functionality of the job itself *and* the personalities involved. It is easier to zero in on one individual – the hero - who may be at the heart of the daily operation rather than the dynamics of the operation itself.

Most team approaches are designed to address individual personalities to make a "better fit" rather than addressing the real issue: the corporate culture. If the individual is not matched to the job on many levels, not only does he/she suffer but the efficacy of outcomes does...especially in a patient care delivery environment. The irony of this is that people apply for and get positions for which they may be ill suited either professionally or personally. HR departments very often take the hiring manager's word as to whether a person will work out.

Mission statements are one thing but often leave the individual out of the equation.

Supervisors in today's market find it uncomfortable to hire an employee who knows more than they do. That necessitates an interdependency that is difficult for a lot of managers. Part of the balancing act we as managers, are expected to perform is keeping effective communication open within our departments. Balancing input without prejudice. How many of us really do that that well?

Chapter 6
OK, So It's a Bad Day

Big deal. Everyone has them and I am no different. Besides, if I let it get to me, they will see I am not handling my job.

Everyone in business today has one of 'those' days. You wake up dreading having to face the same issues over and over with seemingly no resolution. If your staff or your co-workers add to the problem, it is even worse. The worst scenario is if your immediate supervisor is either self-serving or not caring.

I always joked about ADD being a prerequisite for my type of job. I never knew from one hour to the next what was going to happen. Such is the world of health care. The unpredictability of what walks through those doors is what keeps us motivated...we say. More important is the fact that we can face all that uncertainty, pain, disease, and death and keep on going knowing we have helped or even saved one life. That was what kept me going...until...

The day that I cornered the young intern with the script he had written for the wife of one of our VP's (which, if she had taken the meds, could have either killed her or hospitalized her) was an event marker of huge proportion. When he blamed the nurse, I corrected him. When he stated the labs in the medical record showed that the drug was indicated, I asked him to show me the lab results...he could not. He finished, after blaming the system, by blaming me. It was a morning with a board meeting where my "professionals" were throwing verbal barbs and my patience had disappeared earlier that day after a run-in with a doctor who had ignored a patient for two hours.

At that point I lost it. I ended up basically advising the young fellow that he was not only extremely rude and off base but if he expected to be a good physician he needed – at minimum - to research his scripts before he caused a patient harm and check his attitude at the door. I backed off a bit telling him that he accepted responsibility for whatever errors might be in the record by signing that script. The big challenge in medicine is to do right...despite the obstacles.

Upon returning to my office, I told my administrative assistant (St. Marie I called her, for obvious reasons) that I would be leaving for the afternoon and could not be reached. The shock on her face told it all...I had never done that before.

It was a bad day...an unbelievably bad day. The gargoyle had sunk his claws into my shoulder and was not leaving.

I picked up a few papers, tossed them into my briefcase and walking past my admin without looking at her I left my office. I could feel her concern...it was palpable. Once I got in my car, I sat without moving for a while finally putting my head on the steering wheel. A tap on the window startled me bringing me back to life. The parking lot guard was standing next to my car. I put the window down.

"Are you OK?" She was visibly worried.

"Thank you. Just very tired and not feeling too well. I'm heading out."

Chapter 7
Accountability

I could not believe it. The evidence was right there in front of me in black and white. I had missed a detail which would have cost several thousand dollars to fix. I knew I could fix it and make it go away. No one would know…except me. I had caught it in time.

Everyone makes mistakes or overlooks something. I guess I should not have let it get to me; however, I was beginning to feel as though no one day would pass easily. Simply by accepting the responsibility of any job, especially one in a patient care delivery system, one agrees to do the work. What does it take to be good at something which is inherently problematic?

To take care of one patient takes lab technicians, engineers (keeping oxygen flowing/equipment working), each of the nurses on each shift change all the way back to admitting, patient safety staff and even medical records. I guess because this system we call health care takes the interaction of so many people who depend on each other is why the stress can be so consuming.

I have always said that, even in my profession as an administrator, in health care there is no "pass the buck" or "that can wait". One knows whether one's colleague can perform or not...the accountability factor is a heavy weight around each of our shoulders.

Dr. Sanjay Gupta has written a book called "Monday Mornings". It deals with physician conferences on that day to discuss the errors which have occurred during the past week. Because this is an open forum and designed to alert staff to problems rather than place the blame, it is often looked at not as a problem-solving forum but a place the blame on someone game.

In my last position I conducted a scheduled meeting to discuss the week's 'issues'. I was pleased and surprised when my LVN openly admitted he had made a mistake. That kind of honesty is difficult in a profession where excellence is not only expected but demanded…the quality of care and often patient's very lives are at stake.

I had worked hard to have trust built within my staff. What I inherited was something radically different than anything with which I had experienced. From day one I tried hard to let folks know I was not there to accuse or blame but to fix things and keep us on track. I had private meetings with each staff member when I first took that job with a "what is working and what is not" focus. To this day I am sure, probably due to the culture already in place; most were not entirely honest with me.

Due to the emotional/cultural bias, HIV/Primary care on an outpatient basis is probably one of the most difficult patient care delivery systems. Dealing with the inherent issues ranging from patients not taking medications properly to system malfunctions such as labs missing takes a toll on even the most dedicated provider.

Chapter 8
Down

That I had hit the wall, I knew. That I was having a hell of hard day, I knew. What I did not know was that this was only the beginning. Had I known what I was about to go through…well, I am not sure, even today, that I would opt to go there every day but would have simply walked away.

Maslach and Leiter deal with this phenomenon extensively. "Eventually, some people reach a point where they can't take it anymore and they quit. Even when it is necessary, such a decision can be very painful if it means walking away from a career that was once a source of pride, prestige, and personal identity" (*The Truth About Burnout*, Christina Maslach and Michael P. Leiter)

This is exactly where I was in 1995... I quit.

Even years later when the specter again reared its ugly head, I considered simply grabbing my car keys and walking out. That is the thing, you see. You never really let it go completely. If you are honest, you can deal with the vicissitudes of a bad day, but you know that somewhere down there, you are again facing that old, familiar specter.

I reached a point where I would close my office door and tell my secretary to hold all calls. I would shuffle papers and work on mindless projects for hours simply marking time and not even knowing what I was doing.. I simply felt numb. Often, I would take the time to chart the problem trying to find a solution, only to realize the factors involved were beyond my control. I would mentally go off into another place where I could escape, even for a few minutes.

Even with this last venture, after a particularly difficult meeting with a patient or physician, I would go back to my office frustrated asking myself how things could deteriorate to the point where an administrator must sit to facilitate effective communication while a physician rooms a patient. These are supposed to be professionals who are tops in their respective fields. Even the best at times they need a second voice. Yet again, I was dealing with poor communication and egos and not handling it well.

The culture of any organization often dictates the direction one takes when stress takes over. Prior to my acceptance of the position, the environment I was in had changed drastically with key personnel moving on, getting relieved of their positions and, in general, the health care industry itself changing. My position had no one taking charge for, what I was told, was about five years. Additionally, new staff arrived with an "it's all about me" attitude. Current staff were suddenly being held accountable for the first time in years. Quality patient centered care seemed to take a back seat. During a recent conference I attended in Dallas with IHI (Institute of Healthcare Improvement, www.ihi.org), of the 1500 people from Holland, the UK, Italy and the US at that conference, everyone – almost to a person – agreed that the system is broken.

I am not sure when that began, perhaps it always existed and the sheer volume of people moving through it finally exacerbated it to the point where it was visible. Even today I see issues with patient care, EHR (electronic health records) pages being given to the wrong patient, additional medical record numbers assigned to the same patient, medication errors, incorrect diagnosis and burn out of key staff.

The PHI (private healthcare information) aspect of patient care is violated on many levels. Doctors are often not careful when discussing their patient's condition while other patients and families are within earshot. I have personally witnessed a physician sitting with a family in the ED waiting room talking in detail about their relative's condition with ten other people listening. Doctors discuss their patient's prognosis and treatment protocols in hallways, in the cafeteria and even in front of other patients who are in ICU or the ED. Upon being dismissed, a patient's discharge papers have included sheets from some one else's medical record...complete with name, S/S, DX, and treatment protocols.

For the longest time I took it out on myself – still do, to a degree if I am honest. However, burnout is a function of the organization and not the individual. In today's health care environment, it leads to mistakes which can be costly to the organization...but more importantly can put a patient at risk.

Recently having been back into a hospital environment and seeing the mistakes, poor morale and incredible lack of universal precautions gave me real pause about getting back into the field. Having to deal with patient issues on that level is draining when one can do little about it. Hearing the consternation in family member's voices when they get bad news about their loved one's issues is hard. The ED staff, at times can be really pushed and that sometimes comes across as rude. Talking to a grief stricken or scared family is never an easy thing, even for seasoned professionals. It is a two-way street with all the issues...

I vividly remember taking a call from the daughter of a patient. She said she simply wanted us to know her mother had passed. She told me that she brought her mother to the ED with a high fever and night sweats. The staff apparently ran the usual diagnostics, stabilized her mother, gave her a round of antibiotics, and discharged her. Two days later the mother was readmitted to the ED for the same symptoms whereupon the same procedures were repeated...again discharging her.

Three days later, the daughter had to call 911 as her mother had lost consciousness. The EMS crew took her to the closer hospital this time where she passed away several hours later. The daughter indicated she was not going to pursue any malpractice issues even though the latest admission and tests revealed a missed diagnosis. To this day, I do not know why this woman did not pursue that avenue...luckily for the hospital she did not. My level of frustration and helplessness pushed me hard enough, knowing I could do nothing about it other than process the report, to decide that – finally – I would leave health care for good.

If I could have done something, held someone accountable, made a difference...perhaps I would have stayed. Perhaps...

This is but a single example, albeit severe, of the kind of problems coming out of a broken system. Among health care professionals, if they are honest, many will agree that the system is indeed broken.

Why, might you ask? The problems are legion as delivering quality, patient-centered, proactive care is complicated at best.

However, a core issue seems to be burnout.

Chapter 9
Mask Time

Looking in the mirror one morning as I got ready to go to work, I thought I looked fine. *Well, perhaps this will pass after all and I can get back to being me again.*

Walking in my office later that morning, my administrative assistant even said, "Boy, you look better!"

"And a cheery good morning to you to," I joked back. Marie and I had been through a lot together. Opening the hospital was pure hell at times as I recounted to her many times. She was part of my life AFTER the mental barrage of data, politics, and everyday distractions.

I was in such denial that I had a problem. Even to this day I experience denial of sorts. I tell myself that I am so together. The long-term effects of the stress are with me to this day. Life does have a way of moving on; however, the specter still rears its ugly head at the most doggone times...sometimes at three in the morning. The freight train leaves the station at that point and, despite all the "baggage", I jump on it. The plethora of thoughts that get on that train with me take control until I force them back into the dark recesses of my mind...much like I did every day in the middle of the chaos.

Every profession has its quirks, but I think that few can identify with the pressures of opening a hospital and, unfortunately, to this day the ghosts still lurk in the shadows. The challenges ranged from architectural nightmares (doors made for the sterile corridor side of the OR put in on the patient entrance side – too small to get a gurney in), the pit for the lithotripter being too small to accommodate the footprint of the unit actually purchased, ambushes between staffers actually resulting in the firing of a key director, multiple delays with equipment, contractor delays and finally, me being set up in a staff meeting by the directors of three different departments with their own 'agenda'.

Ambushes happen all the time and I am always stunned at the lack of respect shown to fellow workers. Shortly before I left my last job, a staff member (not even on my level), rather than advising me of the importance of a project, went directly to the ED. She simply needed to have asked me for more information. I had been in direct contact with the agency requesting the report. They were advised and agreeable to a revised submission date. Nevertheless, it became an agenda item to be used to my disadvantage.

So, I moved on each day in denial of the things crawling on the tunnel walls of my daily journey trying to focus on what I considered the important thing: opening the hospital to bring a quality care to our patients...was that not what we were there for? In this last venue, again, focusing on the delivery of care, building a staff that could respect each other and work effectively toward a common goal.

Recently with this last foray into health care management, I was beset with the exact same problem ...someone else's priority as it related to mission vs. bottom line. All the ghosts appeared one by one with some of those meetings. I was then, and am now, constantly amazed at how many professionals seem to make knee-jerk decisions without doing due diligence and, at the very least, establish honest communication with those who are on the front lines.

Managers do not always make certain a certain staff member is suited for the job. I think they are afraid to hire those with more expertise than they themselves have in a specific area.

Health care today is fraught with pitfalls and patient safety issues. During a conference in Dallas, I had the privilege of working with several hundred of my peers who, to a person, said that health care delivery systems today are “broken.” I think it is that frustration level that builds with many of us who care more for the lives of those for whom we responsible than the ‘bottom line.’

And…so we move on.

Epilogue

One Foot in Front of the Other – Eyes Ahead

That seems to be what it's all about. Why then is something so simple such a problem for so many of us?

I admire those who can do that, without missing a step and at the same time I wonder if they aren't just a little insane. Interesting concept, huh? Who can go about their routine's day after day after day and be effective…consistently? I know that in theory, that's impossible. No one is perfect all the time. However, they put on a damn good show.

To ask anyone, except my life partner, who knows me at all, I might be described as intelligent, organized, and focused…able to accomplish things. His understanding of me is remarkably different.

He does the dance…day after day. He is damn good at what he does. Although he does describe me as intelligent and organized, it stops very firmly there. Only he has seen the person below all of that. Only he has seen what it costs me to put up that front for any length of time. Oh, I can do it. I can accomplish good things, and even some great things. I was a very integral part of a team that brought a new cancer hospital up online and saw our first patients come in and some leave in remission. What that three-year project alone cost me; I'll never get back. My latest voyage, after retiring for the first time, was being recruited to manage a clinic with 1300 patients who over a six-month period chalked up 7000 visits. I inherited a myriad of problems which had not been addressed for over five years...leaving the raft floating around and bumping into things. I accomplished, I am told, great things and I know I made a difference in the lives of over twenty patients I worked hard to keep in care – or in some cases even getting them into care. I know I saved the lives of at least five others. Little did I know...the balancing act wasn't working...Déjà vu.

The organization thing? Well, that is a huge front. It impresses the heck out of people as to how I can move in, take over and organize their business. It's the only way I can keep on track. My ADD kicks in if I'm in the middle of a messy environment. Multi-task? Boy, can I…for a time.

Focus? I put on a good front, but it's only for periods of time. I am easily bored with things. I have been all my life. Once I know I can do it, have done it or in some cases simply know I can do it, I tune out.

Here comes the one foot in front of the other thing. How DO all of you manage? I don't understand. Am I arrogant? Not a chance. I don't have that high an opinion of myself. I have only just begun to scratch the surface of these things. At my age, I find that totally ludicrous…and more than a little frightening.

If it were not for my partner, I might not have been putting that "one foot in front of the other". He's been my alpha and my omega. He's seen me at my worst and my best. I hope I give him most of what he needs. I love him with all my heart. Who knows that if I were alone, I might have coped better? Part of me is scared to death that isn't the case. I know I am a survivor, but still…

Therefore, this book has emerged out of something very deep inside of me. It is something that, to this day, I am still afraid of letting out. I keep it locked very securely away. My need? My shortcomings? My inability to be aggressive with those who are dishonest or pushing their self-serving agendae? My lack of confidence in that I know I am good at what I do. I'm certain it's from all the above and more.

Under all the bravado we all put forth, I cannot help but feel there is a very insecure little kid in each of us who is at times scared as hell. Were it not for my faith and, not to be trite, the love of a good man, I simply don't know...I just don't know?

I have - since starting this journey writing this book - found that putting everything in print not only makes it real but gives me a better understanding of that phase of my life. I can now pull back and look on as an observer. Were it not for my too trusting nature and inability to accept that not everyone is a good person in this world, would I probably still be running that clinic? Nice guys don't always finish last. However, it is a good thing as my life is now again my own and I have time to go into that dark room without fear where I hid things knowing I can now take them and walk back into the sun.

The lesson to be learned here is the "bucket of water" syndrome. Life goes on without us. Our jobs are filled by others after our departure. The organization goes on. If we forget that, we lose. We are not our jobs, no matter how much we gain from them.

We can make significant contributions...while we are there. We can change lives...while we are there. But never lose sight of the fact that corporations, businesses, partnerships of all kinds go on without us. We are more than just a job title.

The collateral damage is not apparent until it reaches critical mass and is no longer secret...either to ourselves or to those around us.

The more we put our work first and our personal lives second – without balance, the more we risk. That balancing act is hard to achieve for so many of us...and at times the more we try, the more we are in denial...

Geoffrey Zamboni

www.ingramcontent.com/pod-product-compliance
Lightning Source LLC
LaVergne TN
LVHW050924210926
848482LV00012B/530
* 9 7 9 8 8 9 3 9 5 1 6 3 9 *